M000042674

EVERY
TEAR
WILL BE
WIPED
AWAY

*prayers for comfort
in times of grief*

Selected and Introduced by
GRETCHEN L. SCHWENKER, PhD

Liguori
LIGUORI, MISSOURI

Imprimi Potest:
Harry Grile, CSsR, Provincial
Denver Province, The Redemptorists

Published by Liguori Publications
Liguori, Missouri 63057

To order, call 800-325-9521
www.liguori.org

Copyright © 2011 Gretchen L. Schwenker

All rights reserved. No part of this publication may be reproduced, stored in a retrieval system, or transmitted in any form or by any means—electronic, mechanical, photocopy, recording, or any other—except for brief quotations in printed reviews, without the prior written permission of Liguori Publications.

Library of Congress Cataloging-in-Publication Data

Schwenker, Gretchen L.
  Every tear will be wiped away : prayers for comfort in times of grief / Gretchen L. Schwenker.—1st ed.
    p. cm.
  ISBN 978-0-7648-2037-3
1. Grief—Prayers and devotions. 2. Bereavement—Prayers and devotions. 3. Catholic Church—Prayers and devotions. I. Title.
  BX2373.B47S39 2011
  242'.4—dc23

                                                                2011027228

Scripture texts in this work are taken from the *New American Bible,* revised edition © 2010, 1991, 1986, 1970 Confraternity of Christian Doctrine, Inc., Washington, DC. All Rights Reserved.

Excerpts from *Order of Christian Funerals* © 1985, International Committee on English in the Liturgy, Inc. (ICEL); excerpts from the English translation of *The Roman Missal* © 2010, ICEL. All rights reserved.

Compliant with *The Roman Missal,* third edition.

Liguori Publications, a nonprofit corporation, is an apostolate of the Redemptorists. To learn more about the Redemptorists, visit Redemptorists.com.

Printed in the United States of America
15 14 13 12 11 / 5 4 3 2 1
First Edition

CONTENTS

INTRODUCTION

Living through grief takes courage. When we lose someone we love, everything we know alters dramatically. Because our lives change so significantly, constancy is what we need most. For Christians, faith may be the best source of that constancy. Faith can provide the sense of security that enables us to enter into a dialogue with deep loss, helps us cope with the pain, and in time, even remake our lives.

Getting through feelings of loss is a process. Even as we mourn, we Christians are consoled in our belief that death is only a separation, not an end. Our faith comforts us because we know our beloved dead are given a new beginning—a life more fully experienced with God. This realization does not take away our grief, but it

does provide solace. As our journey continues, it can lead us to a spirit of joyful hope. We can also come to understand that having known our beloved is a gift that will always remain with us. We can begin to feel genuine gratitude.

Our gratitude comes most deeply from understanding that all life has been given to us freely and generously by a loving God. This unconditional love, which knows no limits, helps raise us out of personal distress. As Saint Paul reminds us, love "endures all things," even death. Our faith gives us the strength to endure a serious loss because we know we are not alone. Christ is the center of our lives, and we can overcome any hardship—even the death of a loved one—because of our life in the Risen Lord. It is not that we forget our loss, but we see it in a new way—through the eyes of faith. This deeper perspective can provide peace and enable us to go on.

Thus in gratitude and strengthened by the Holy Spirit, we can stand firm in our faith, using the remainder of our lives to reflect God's love to others. We who have loved have been blessed. In return, our faith calls us to be a blessing to others, and this becomes possible when we make the effort to live a life of prayerful reflection.

Prayer can be a constant touchstone as we make our way through grief. In communion with God, we grow in gratitude and are made stronger. When we pray, we open ourselves to the work of the Holy Spirit and God's transforming presence in our lives. We allow the Spirit to guide our hearts and bring enlightenment to our being. We learn to hear God in the silence beyond the words of prayer. It is in responding to what we hear that we are changed. Prayer renews our spirit, freeing us of whatever obscures our path toward a more Christ-centered life.

Our prayer can praise God, express gratitude, and seek forgiveness, but we can also petition God when we are in trouble, asking for assistance and support. This petitioning is the most common form of prayer, and it is a safe way to speak

our truth, whatever it may be. Healing can begin in this kind of conversation with God.

When we try to make sense of our lives without someone we dearly valued and when our grief seems overwhelming, prayer can offer consolation. Coping with grief after the death of someone close to us can take some time, and there is no formula. We can find the will to continue through our faith, but our heart may still hold a brokenness within from that loss. Making room for prayer on a regular basis—and allowing the silence that is part of our dialogue with God to envelop us—can nevertheless help mend that brokenness as we move through grief. Sometimes prayer can offer revelation as we receive the wisdom to see beyond our own story. Suddenly our focus shows us more clearly what we are called to do. Prayer widens our hearts so that we can recognize the needs of others and respond to their needs in love. Ultimately, prayer can bring us deep joy.

During the more than two thousand years

since Jesus lived among us, we have found ourselves made better by following him and listening to the Word of God, our Bible. Praying with Scripture regularly can give us a greater understanding of everything God has done for us, as well as everything we are asked to do in return. Beyond the Bible, we have a wealth of ancient traditional prayers from which to draw, including those from our liturgy. Finally, we can look to generations of witnesses to our faith who have led by their fidelity. They have modeled for us how God does hear our prayers; these prayers are answered—we are never alone— even though the outcome may not be what we had hoped.

The prayers and reflections in this book are intended to help sustain you through grief and the pain and sadness that mark it. Certain prayers may speak to your feelings better than other prayers, just as particular lines or words may es-

pecially give you focus. However you pray with these prayers is as individual as your own story.

This book is divided into four parts that are meant to help you on the journey through your personal experience of loss and help you move to a stronger faith, hope, and love.

In the first part, we seek to petition God for aid—"Hear our prayer."

This is followed by prayers offering consolation—"Every tear will be wiped away."

Next are prayers reminding us of the promise of heaven—"May angels lead you into paradise."

Finally, prayers are included that will evoke that homecoming—"Glory of all believers."

For scriptural passages other than psalms, new companion prayers have been provided to aid your spiritual reflection.

In closing, the epilogue visits the stages of grief as outlined by Elisabeth Kübler-Ross. An appendix also offers several litanies from deep within the Christian tradition, including the Litany of the Saints and the Litany of Saint Joseph.

Our prayer is that someday all of us will see those we love again when we too are called home to the Lord. May they rest in peace, and God give you peace.

HEAR OUR PRAYER

To choose life means to embrace the cross. It means to put up with the cross, the difficulties, the lack of success, the fear of standing alone. Tradition has never promised us a rose garden. To embrace the cross today means to grow into resistance. And the cross will turn green and blossom. We survive the cross. We grow in suffering. We are the tree of life.

DOROTHEE SOELLE

And I tell you, ask and you will receive; seek and you will find; knock and the door will be opened to you.

For everyone who asks, receives; and the one who seeks, finds; and to the one who knocks, the door will be opened.

LUKE 11:9–10

Merciful God, hear us.
Listen to our prayers, now and forever.
In times of sorrow,
we seek your loving aid.
Let us never cease to call on you,
asking help and comfort.
Let us always find you.
We give thanks and praise to you,
who will not turn us away.
Amen.

GRETCHEN L. SCHWENKER

O merciful God, who answerest the poor,
   Answer us,
O merciful God, who answerest
      the lowly in spirit,
   Answer us,
O merciful God, who answerest
      the broken of heart,
   Answer us.
O merciful God,
   Answer us.
O merciful God,
   Have compassion.
O merciful God,
   Redeem.
O merciful God,
   Save.
O merciful God, have pity upon us,
   Now,
   Speedily,
   And at a near time.

—JEWISH PRAYER, DAY OF ATONEMENT

Memorare

Remember, O most gracious Virgin Mary,

that never was it known

that anyone who fled to your protection,

implored your help,

or sought your intercession

was left unaided.

Inspired with this confidence,

I fly to you, O Virgin of virgins, my Mother.

To you I come,

before you I stand, sinful and sorrowful.

O Mother of the Word Incarnate,

despise not my petitions,

but in your mercy,

hear and answer me.

Amen.

My life is deprived of peace,
I have forgotten what happiness is;
My enduring hope, I said,
has perished before the LORD....

But this I will call to mind;
therefore I will hope:
The LORD's acts of mercy are not exhausted,
his compassion is not spent;
They are renewed each morning—
great is your faithfulness!
The LORD is my portion, I tell myself;
therefore I will hope in him.

The LORD is good to those who trust in him,
to the one that seeks him;
It is good to hope in silence
for the LORD's deliverance.

LAMENTATIONS 3:17–18, 21–26

We call on you, Lord.
On you we can rely
when peace seems gone,
our hearts broken by sadness.
Grant us your compassion,
lifting us back into life.
So we may serve you in joy,
each new morning we wake.
Amen.

GRETCHEN L. SCHWENKER

Incline your ear, LORD, and answer me,
    for I am poor and oppressed.
Preserve my life, for I am devoted;
    save your servant who trusts in you.
You are my God; be gracious to me, Lord;
    to you I call all the day.
Gladden the soul of your servant;
    to you, Lord, I lift up my soul.
Lord, you are good and forgiving,
    most merciful to all who call on you.
LORD, hear my prayer;
    listen to my cry for help.
On the day of my distress I call to you,
    for you will answer me.

PSALM 86:1–7

Our Father,
You would not willingly call on us
　　to suffer.
You say all things work together
　　for our good
if we are faithful to You.
Therefore, if You ordain it:
through disappointment and poverty,
sickness and pain,
even shame and contempt
　　and calumny,
You will support us with the
consolation of Your Grace
and compensate us
for any temporal suffering
by the possession of that peace
which the world can neither give
　　nor take away.

SAINT ELIZABETH ANN SETON

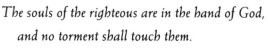

The souls of the righteous are in the hand of God,
*   and no torment shall touch them.*
They seemed, in the view of the foolish, to be dead;
*   and their passing away was thought an affliction*
*   and their going forth from us, utter destruction.*
But they are in peace.
For if to others, indeed, they seem punished,
*   yet is their hope full of immortality;*
Chastised a little, they shall be greatly blessed,
*   because God tried them*
*   and found them worthy of himself.*
As gold in the furnace, he proved them,
*   and as sacrificial offerings he took them to himself.*
In the time of their judgment they shall shine,
*   and dart about as sparks through stubble;*
They shall judge nations and rule over peoples,
*   and the LORD shall be their King forever.*
Those who trust in him shall understand truth,
*   and the faithful shall abide with him in love:*
Because grace and mercy are with his holy ones,
*   and his care is with the elect.*

WISDOM 3:1–9

Remember, Lord, your faithful,
those souls of the righteous
whom you found worthy.
Receive our beloved dead,
taking them to yourself.
Now freed of every torment,
bless them with your love;
your truth revealed in new life.
Give us grace who feel
alone without them,
trusting in your infinite care.

GRETCHEN L. SCHWENKER

O Lord, you have made us very small, and we bring our years to an end like a tale that is told.

Help us to remember that beyond our brief day is the eternity of your love.

REINHOLD NIEBUHR

O my God! I ask of you for myself and for those whom I hold dear, the grace to fulfill perfectly your holy will, to accept for love of you the joys and sorrows of this passing life, so that we may one day be united together in heaven for all Eternity. Amen.

SAINT THÉRÈSE OF LISIEUX

My eyes are ever upon the LORD,
   who frees my feet from the snare.
Look upon me, have pity on me,
   for I am alone and afflicted.
Relieve the troubles of my heart;
   bring me out of my distress.
Look upon my affliction and suffering;
   take away all my sins.

PSALM 25:15–18

Christ our eternal King and God, You have destroyed death and the devil by Your Cross and have restored man to life by Your Resurrection; give rest, Lord, to the soul of Your servant who has fallen asleep, in Your Kingdom, where there is no pain, sorrow or suffering. In Your goodness and love for all men, pardon all the sins he (she) has committed in thought, word or deed, for there is no man or woman who lives and sins not, You only are without sin.

For You are the Resurrection, the Life, and Repose of Your servant, departed this life, O Christ our God; and to You do we send up glory with Your Eternal Father and Your All-holy, Good and Life-creating Spirit; both now and forever and to the ages of ages. Amen.

FROM *THE DIVINE LITURGY OF
ST. JOHN CHRYSOSTOM*

Oh Holy Spirit, come into my heart;
by your power draw it to yourself, God,
and give me charity with fear.
Guard me, Christ, from every evil
thought,
and so warm and enflame me again
with your most gentle love
that every suffering may seem light to me.
My holy Father and my gentle Lord,
help me in my every need!
Christ love! Christ love!

SAINT CATHERINE OF SIENA

When Mary came to where Jesus was and saw him, she fell at his feet and said to him, "Lord, if you had been here, my brother would not have died." When Jesus saw her weeping and the Jews who had come with her weeping, he became perturbed and deeply troubled, and said, "Where have you laid him?" They said to him, "Sir, come and see." And Jesus wept. So the Jews said, "See how he loved him." But some of them said, "Could not the one who opened the eyes of the blind man have done something so that this man would not have died?"

So Jesus, perturbed again, came to the tomb. It was a cave, and a stone lay across it. Jesus said, "Take away the stone." Martha, the dead man's sister, said to him, "Lord, by now there will be a stench; he has been dead for four days."

Jesus said to her, "Did I not tell you that if you believe you will see the glory of God?" So they took away the stone. And Jesus raised his eyes and said, "Father, I thank you for hearing me. I know that you always hear me; but because of the crowd here I have said this, that they may believe that you sent

me." And when he had said this, he cried out in a loud voice, "Lazarus, come out!" The dead man came out, tied hand and foot with burial bands, and his face was wrapped in a cloth. So Jesus said to them, "Untie him and let him go."

JOHN 11:32–44

Dear Lord Jesus, keep me strong.
Renew my faith even in grief.
You wept for Lazarus.
You know the human heart,
how easily it breaks.
Let me turn to God, the Father,
believing that he hears me.
Let me turn to you, embracing
the promise of eternal life.
Amen.

GRETCHEN L. SCHWENKER

Govern all by your wisdom, O Lord, so that my soul may always be serving you as you will and not as I choose....Let me die to myself that I may serve you. Let me live to you who in yourself are the true life.

SAINT TERESA OF ÁVILA

EVERY TEAR WILL BE
WIPED AWAY

The real lesson of resurrection may be its strangest, strongest one. When Jesus died, hope died. The apostles grieved the death of Jesus. The public was scandalized. The synagogue said good riddance to a troublemaker. The entire enterprise collapsed. But in the end, out of apparent failure, came new life stronger than it had ever been before. And so, too, for us. When one phase of life ends, a new one arises, if we do not spend too much time grieving the one before it, if we allow new grace to flow through us, if we accept the fact that "the third day"—the moment of ultimate incidents—is an ordinary moment of time turned Christic, turned salvific, turned new.

JOAN CHITTISTER

It is truly right and just,

    our duty and our salvation,

always and everywhere to give you thanks,

Lord, holy Father, almighty and eternal God,

through Christ our Lord.

In him the hope of blessed resurrection

    has dawned,

that those saddened by the certainty of dying

might be consoled by the promise of

    immortality to come.

Indeed for your faithful, Lord,

life is changed not ended,

and, when this earthly dwelling turns to dust,

an eternal dwelling is made ready for them

    in heaven.

PREFACE I FOR THE DEAD, ROMAN MISSAL

The eyes of the Lord are directed toward the righteous
and his ears toward their cry....
The righteous cry out, the LORD hears
and he rescues them from all their afflictions.
The LORD is close to the brokenhearted,
saves those whose spirit is crushed.
Many are the troubles of the righteous,
but the LORD delivers him from them all.

PSALM 34:16, 18–20

Morning Prayers (excerpts)

O God, early in the morning I cry to you.
Help me to pray
And to concentrate my thoughts on you;
I cannot do this alone.

In me there is darkness,
But with you there is light;
I am lonely, but you do not leave me;
I am feeble in heart, but with you there is help;
I am restless, but with you there is peace.
In me there is bitterness,
   but with you there is patience;
I do not understand your ways,
But you know the way for me.

Lord Jesus Christ,
You were poor
and in distress, a captive and forsaken as I am.
You know all man's troubles;

You abide with me
when all men fail me;
You remember and seek me;
It is your will that I should know you
and turn to you.
Lord, I hear your call and follow;
Help me.

DIETRICH BONHOEFFER

Then I saw a new heaven and a new earth. The former heaven and the former earth had passed away, and the sea was no more. I also saw the holy city, a new Jerusalem, coming down out of heaven from God, prepared as a bride adorned for her husband. I heard a loud voice from the throne saying, "Behold, God's dwelling is with the human race. He will dwell with them and they will be his people and God himself will always be with them [as their God]. He will wipe every tear from their eyes, and there shall be no more death or mourning, wailing or pain, [for] the old order has passed away."

The one who sat on the throne said, "Behold I make all things new....To the thirsty I will give a gift from the spring of life-giving water. The victor will inherit these gifts, and I shall be his God, and he will be my son."

REVELATION 21:1-5A, 6B-7A

In mourning, I seek you, my God.
Give me vision to see your holy city,
to realize that you are always with me,
healing my pain and distress,
stopping these tears of loss.
You are life-giving water,
reviving my soul,
leading me home to your care,
granting me victory over death.
Amen.

GRETCHEN L. SCHWENKER

Watch, dear Lord,
with those who wake, or watch,
    or weep tonight,
and give your angels charge over those
    who sleep.
Tend your sick ones, O Lord Jesus Christ,
rest your weary ones.
Bless your dying ones.
Soothe your suffering ones.
Pity your afflicted ones.
Shield your joyous ones.
And all for your love's sake,
Amen.

SAINT AUGUSTINE

O God, you care for your creation with great tenderness. In the midst of overwhelming pain, you offer hope. Give help to me, whose spirit seems to be lost and whose soul is in despair. Let me feel your love. Let me believe in a rebirth of joy so that I can experience now a small taste of the happiness I wish to know in eternity. Amen.

DIMMA, SEVENTH-CENTURY IRISH MONK

Come to me, all you who labor and are burdened, and I will give you rest. Take my yoke upon you and learn from me, for I am meek and humble of heart; and you will find rest for yourselves. For my yoke is easy, and my burden light.

MATTHEW 11:28–30

Gentle savior, who is my strength,
save me from being overwhelmed
by this burden of loss
that crushes my spirit,
leaving me without rest.
Bring me close to you,
carry me along
into the lightness of being
that is your heart.
Amen.

GRETCHEN L. SCHWENKER

For Healing

Lord, you invite all who are burdened
    to come to you.
Allow Your healing Hand to heal me.
Touch my soul with Your compassion
    for others;
touch my heart with Your courage
and infinite Love for all;
touch my mind with Your Wisdom,
and may my mouth always proclaim Your
    praise.
Teach me to reach out to You in all my
    needs,
and help me to lead others to You by my
    example.

Most loving Heart of Jesus,
bring me health in body and spirit
that I may serve You with all my strength.
Touch gently this life which You have
    created,
now and forever. Amen.

Out of the depths I call to you, LORD;
*   Lord, hear my cry!*
May your ears be attentive
*   to my cry for mercy.*
If you, LORD, keep account of sins,
*   Lord, who can stand?*
But with you is forgiveness
*   and so you are revered.*

I wait for the LORD,
*   my soul waits*
*   and I hope for his word.*
My soul looks for the Lord
*   more than sentinels for daybreak.*
More than sentinels for daybreak,
*   let Israel hope in the LORD,*
For with the LORD is mercy,
*   with him is plenteous redemption,*
And he will redeem Israel
*   from all its sins.*

PSALM 130:1–8

Soon afterward he journeyed to a city called Nain, and his disciples and a large crowd accompanied him. As he drew near to the gate of the city, a man who had died was being carried out, the only son of his mother, and she was a widow. A large crowd from the city was with her. When the Lord saw her, he was moved with pity for her and said to her, "Do not weep." He stepped forward and touched the coffin; at this the bearers halted, and he said, "Young man, I tell you, arise!" The dead man sat up and began to speak, and Jesus gave him to his mother.

LUKE 7:11–15

Lord Jesus, my sorrow engulfs me.
Yet I know that you are there,
as you have always been,
as you always will be,
taking care of those in need.
Let me know your healing touch,
help me cast off my grief,
knowing that all will rise again
in your redeeming love.
Amen.

GRETCHEN L. SCHWENKER

O Lord Jesus Christ, Whose Name is called Counsellor, give us grace, I beseech Thee, always to hear and obey Thy Voice which saith to every one of us, "This is the way, walk ye in it." Nevertheless, let us not hear It behind us saying, This is the way; but rather before us saying, Follow Me. When Thou puttest us forth, go before us; when the way is too great for us, carry us; in the darkness of death, comfort us; in the day of resurrection, satisfy us. Amen.

CHRISTINA ROSSETTI

Lord, Jesus Christ

Thou Son of the Most High, Prince of Peace, be born again into our world. Wherever there is war in this world, wherever there is pain, wherever there is loneliness, wherever there is no hope, come, thou long-expected one, with healing in thy wings.

Holy Child, whom the shepherds and the kings and the dumb beasts adored, be born again. Wherever there is boredom, wherever there is fear of failure, wherever there is temptation too strong to resist, wherever there is bitterness of heart, come, thou blessed one, with healing in thy wings.

Saviour, be born in each of us who raises his face to thy face, not knowing fully who he is or who thou art, knowing only that thy love is beyond his knowing and that no other has the power to make him whole. Come, Lord Jesus, to each who longs for thee even though he has forgotten thy name. Come quickly. Amen.

FREDERICK BUECHNER

On this mountain the LORD of hosts
  will provide for all peoples....
On this mountain he will destroy
  the veil that veils all peoples,
The web that is woven over all nations.
  He will destroy death forever.
The Lord GOD will wipe away
  the tears from all faces;
The reproach of his people he will remove
  from the whole earth; for the LORD has spoken.
  On that day it will be said:
"Indeed, this is our God; we looked to
    him, and he saved us!
  This is the LORD to whom we looked;
  let us rejoice and be glad that he has saved us!"

ISAIAH 25:6A, 7–9

When I weep, Lord, come to me.
Help me see that you always provide.
Make me realize that you prevail over all,
that nothing, not even death,
is stronger than your love.
Let the whole earth know your greatness.
You have saved us from all misery.
We rejoice in you, our merciful God.
Amen.

GRETCHEN L. SCHWENKER

Remember your servant (name)
whom you have called (today)
from this world to yourself.
Grant that he (she) who was united with your
    Son in a death like his,
may also be one with him in his Resurrection,
when from the earth
he will raise up in the flesh those who have
    died,
and transform our lowly body
after the pattern of his own glorious body.
To our departed brothers and sisters, too,
and to all who were pleasing to you
at their passing from this life,
give kind admittance to your kingdom.
There we hope to enjoy for ever the fullness
    of your glory,
when you will wipe away every tear from our
    eyes.

For seeing you, our God, as you are,

we shall be like you for all the ages

and praise you without end,

through Christ our Lord,

through whom you bestow on the world

    all that is good.

FROM EUCHARISTIC PRAYER III
(FOR MASSES FOR THE DEAD),
THE ROMAN MISSAL

MAY ANGELS LEAD YOU
INTO PARADISE

Heaven knows terrible things happen to people in this world. The good die young, and the wicked prosper, and in any one town, anywhere, there is grief enough to freeze the blood. But from deep within whatever the hidden spring is that life wells up from, there wells up into our lives, even at their darkest and maybe especially then, a power to heal, to breathe new life into us.

FREDERICK BUECHNER

Kontakion 9

Bless swiftly passing time: every hour, every moment bringeth eternity nearer to us. A new sorrow, a new gray hair are heralds of the world to come, they are witnesses of earthly corruption, they proclaim that all passeth away, that the eternal kingdom draweth nigh, where there are neither tears, nor sighing, but the joyful song: Alleluia!

Ikos 9

As a tree loseth its leaves little by little, so also our days, with each year, decline into weakness. The festival of youth fadeth. The lamp of rejoicing is extinguished, the isolation of old age approacheth, friends and family die. Where are the young merrymakers, joyful and happy? Silent are their tombs, but their souls are in Thy hand; their glances are felt from the world beyond the grave.*

*Akathist hymns come from the Eastern Orthodox and Eastern Catholic churches and are sung to a saint, a Person of the Trinity, or to commemorate a holy event. "Akathist" refers to the standing of the people while the hymn is sung, manifesting reverence for the icon. The most famous of all akathist hymns is to the Theotokos (meaning "God-bearer," ancient title given to the Blessed Virgin, Mother of God). Kontakion and Ikos are two of several elements that make up an akathist hymn.

I am going now into the sleep,
Be it that I in health shall wake;
If death be to me in deathly sleep,
Be it that in thine own arm's keep,
O God of grace, to new life I wake;
O be it in thy dear arm's keep,
O God of grace, that I shall awake!

—FROM *POEMS OF THE
WESTERN HIGHLANDERS* (1900)

O bodiless Angels, as you stand before God's throne, and are enlightened by its rays, and with the overflow of light forever shining, pray to Christ to give our souls peace and grant us mercy.

LORD, I CALL

In paradisum (*Into paradise*)

In paradisum deducant te Angeli;
in tuo adventu suscipiant te martyres,
et perducant te in civitatem sanctam Ierusalem.
Chorus angelorum te suscipiat,
et cum Lazaro quondam paupere æternam
habeas requiem.

May the angels lead you into paradise,
May the martyrs receive you at your coming
And bring you into the holy city,
    into Jerusalem.
May a choir of angels welcome you;
And there, where Lazarus is poor no longer,
May you have eternal rest.

ANTIPHON, LATIN LITURGY, REQUIEM MASS

For those who are led by the Spirit of God are children of God. For you did not receive a spirit of slavery to fall back into fear, but you received a spirit of adoption, through which we cry, "Abba, Father!" The Spirit itself bears witness with our spirit that we are children of God, and if children, then heirs, heirs of God and joint heirs with Christ, if only we suffer with him so that we may also be glorified with him. I consider that the sufferings of this present time are as nothing compared with the glory to be revealed for us.

ROMANS 8:14–18

Heavenly Father,
let me live as your child.
Help me accept suffering,
united with your Son.
Let me abandon loneliness
and live instead in the Spirit,
trusting in the revelation
of your glory. Amen.

GRETCHEN L. SCHWENKER

Into your hands, O Lord,
we humbly entrust our brother/sister
　　(name).
In this life you embraced him/her
　　with your tender love;
deliver him/her now from every evil
and bid him/her enter eternal rest.

The old order has passed away;
welcome him/her then into paradise,
where there will be no sorrow,
　　no weeping nor pain,
but the fullness of peace and joy
with your Son and the Holy Spirit
forever and ever.
Amen.

RITE OF GATHERING
IN THE PRESENCE OF THE BODY,
ORDER OF CHRISTIAN FUNERALS

Are they not all Ministering Spirits?

Lord, whomsoever Thou shalt send to me,
Let that same be
    Mine Angel predilect:
Veiled or unveiled, benignant or austere,
Aloof or near;
    Thine, therefore mine, elect.

So may my soul nurse patience day by day,
Watch on and pray
    Obedient and at peace;
Living a lonely life in hope, in faith;
Loving till death,
    When life, not love, shall cease.

…Lo, thou mine Angel with transfigured face
Brimful of grace,
    Brimful of love for me!
Did I misdoubt thee all that weary while,
Thee with a smile
    For me as I for thee?

CHRISTINA ROSSETTI

I heard a voice from heaven say, "Write this:
Blessed are the dead who die in the Lord from
now on." "Yes," said the Spirit, "let them
find rest from their labors, for their works
accompany them."

REVELATION 14:13

Most gracious Lord,
help us venerate our dead,
these souls we love,
so blessed in their devotion to you,
whose good works helped
reveal your Kingdom on earth.
May we follow them,
witnessing in your name,
as they have before us.
May we know our call
through the Spirit
to labor on until we also
come to rest in you.

GRETCHEN L. SCHWENKER

Welcome Into Heaven

Receive, Lord, the souls of your servants who come home to you. Clothe them with a heavenly garment and wash them in the holy fountain of everlasting life, so that they may be glad with the glad, wise with the wise.

Let them take their seats among the crowned martyrs, move among the patriarchs and prophets, and follow Christ in the company of the apostles.

Let them contemplate the splendor of God among the angels and archangels; let them rejoice within the gleaming walks of paradise; let them have knowledge of the divine mysteries and find the brightness of God among the cherubim and seraphim.

Let them wash their robes together with those who wash their garments in the fountain of lights; and knocking, find the gates of heavenly Jerusalem open to them. Let them see God face to face in that company, and savor the ineffable strains of celestial music. Amen.

Anima Christi

Soul of Christ, sanctify me.

Body of Christ, save me.

Blood of Christ, inebriate me.

Water from the side of Christ, wash me.

Passion of Christ, strengthen me.

O good Jesus, hear me.

Within your wounds hide me.

Permit me not to be separated from you.

From the malicious enemy defend me.

In the hour of my death call me.

And bid me come to you,

that with your saints I may praise you

forever and ever. Amen.

We do not want you to be unaware, brothers, about those who have fallen asleep, so that you may not grieve like the rest, who have no hope. For if we believe that Jesus died and rose, so too will God, through Jesus, bring with him those who have fallen asleep. Indeed, we tell you this, on the word of the Lord, that we who are alive, who are left until the coming of the Lord, will surely not precede those who have fallen asleep. For the Lord himself, with a word of command, with the voice of an archangel and with the trumpet of God, will come down from heaven, and the dead in Christ will rise first. Then we who are alive, who are left, will be caught up together with them in the clouds to meet the Lord in the air. Thus we shall always be with the Lord. Therefore, console one another with these words.

1 THESSALONIANS 4:13–18

We turn to our saving Lord,
for strength when we falter,
for faith when grief is deep.
We seek consolation
as life seems no more,
as hope fades in sorrow,
those dear to us gone.
God, through Jesus,
bring them home to you.
Let us take heart, knowing
we will see each other again,
alive in your love.
Amen.

GRETCHEN L. SCHWENKER

When he saw the crowds, he went up the mountain,
and after he had sat down, his disciples came to him.
He began to teach them, saying:
"Blessed are the poor in spirit,
    for theirs is the kingdom of heaven.
Blessed are they who mourn,
    for they will be comforted.
Blessed are the meek, for they will inherit the land.
Blessed are they who hunger and thirst for
    righteousness, for they will be satisfied.
Blessed are the merciful, for they will be shown mercy.
Blessed are the clean of heart, for they will see God.
Blessed are the peacemakers,
    for they will be called children of God.
Blessed are they who are persecuted for the sake of
    righteousness, for theirs is the kingdom of heaven.
Blessed are you when they insult you and persecute
you and utter every kind of evil against you [falsely]
because of me. Rejoice and be glad, for your reward
will be great in heaven."

MATTHEW 5:1–12A

Heal me, Lord Jesus,
even as I mourn deeply.
Fill me with gratitude
for your enveloping love.
You have called me blessed,
opening your heart to me
among many who have lived
by honoring God, our Father.
Keep me ever on that path
toward heaven and joy.
Amen.

GRETCHEN L. SCHWENKER

As the rain hides the stars,
as the autumn mist hides the hills,
as the clouds veil the blue of the sky,
so the dark happenings of my lot
hide the shining of thy face from me.
Yet, if I may hold thy hand
   in the darkness,
it is enough.
Since I know that,
   though I may stumble in my going,
thou dost not fall.

GAELIC PRAYER, ALISTAIR MACLEAN, TRANS.

GLORY OF ALL BELIEVERS

The Freedom of Christians

Paul declares that through Christ we are made free for freedom. Ultimately this freedom is not the absence of forces which determine our existence.... But for us who were born without being asked, who will die without being asked, and who have received a quite definite realm of existence without being asked, a realm which ultimately cannot be exchanged, there is no immediate freedom in the sense of an absence of any and every force which co-determines our existence. But a Christian believes that there is a path to freedom which lies in

going through this imprisonment. We do not seize it by force, but rather it is given to us by God insofar as he gives himself to us throughout all of the imprisonments of our existence.

KARL RAHNER

Prayer of Solace

O Lord, support us all the day long,
until the shadows lengthen
and the evening comes,
and the busy world is hushed,
and the fever of life is over
and our work is done.
Then in thy mercy
grant us a safe lodging,
and a holy rest, and peace at the last.
Amen.

Kontakion 12

Flesh and blood shall not inherit the kingdom of God. However long we live in the flesh we are separated from Christ, but if we die we live for eternity. Our corruptible body must put on incorruption, so that in the light of the unwaning day we may sing: Alleluia!

Ikos 12

We await the meeting with the Lord, we await the bright dawn of the Resurrection, we expect the raising of our near and dear ones from the tombs and the restoration of the dead to the most reverent beauty of life.

We triumph in the coming transfiguration of all creation and cry to our Creator: O Lord, Who didst create the world for the triumph of joy and goodness, Who hast raised us up to holiness out of the depths of sin, grant the dead to reign in the midst of the new creation, that they may shine in heaven on the day of their glory.

O Lord, let the Divine Lamb be to them the unwaning light.

O Lord, grant us also to celebrate with them a Pascha (Passover) incorruptible; unite the dead and the living in unending joy.

O Lord of unutterable love, remember Thy servants who have fallen asleep!*

See note on page 51.

"Do not let your hearts be troubled. You have faith in God; have faith also in me. In my Father's house there are many dwelling places. If there were not, would I have told you that I am going to prepare a place for you? And if I go and prepare a place for you, I will come back again and take you to myself, so that where I am you also may be. Where [I] am going you know the way." Thomas said to him, "Master, we do not know where you are going; how can we know the way?" Jesus said to him, "I am the way and the truth and the life. No one comes to the Father except through me."

JOHN 14:1–6

Sometimes my heart is troubled,
especially by suffering and grief.
Ease those emotions, Lord.
Help me to see beyond here
when I feel distressed or afraid.
You are the way in this life;
let me have faith in you.
Let me believe you have guided
my beloved dead to the Father,
and will return to bring us all
to his house in truth and glory.
Amen.

GRETCHEN L. SCHWENKER

Good Lord, give me the grace so as to spend my life, that when the day of my death shall come, though I feel pain in my body, I may feel comfort in my soul; and with the faithful hope of your mercy, with all the love that is due to you, and with charity toward the world, I may, through your grace, depart into your everlasting glory. Amen.

SAINT THOMAS MORE

The Lord is my shepherd;
    there is nothing I lack.
In green pastures he makes me lie down;
    to still waters he leads me;
    he restores my soul.
He guides me along right paths
    for the sake of his name.
Even though I walk through the valley of
    the shadow of death,
    I will fear no evil, for you are with me;
    your rod and your staff comfort me.

You set a table before me
    in front of my enemies;
You anoint my head with oil;
    my cup overflows.
Indeed, goodness and mercy will pursue me
    all the days of my life;
I will dwell in the house of the LORD
    for endless days.

PSALM 23:1–6

When the sabbath was over, Mary Magdalene, Mary, the mother of James, and Salome bought spices so that they might go and anoint him. Very early when the sun had risen, on the first day of the week, they came to the tomb. They were saying to one another, "Who will roll back the stone for us from the entrance to the tomb?" When they looked up, they saw that the stone had been rolled back; it was very large. On entering the tomb they saw a young man sitting on the right side, clothed in a white robe, and they were utterly amazed. He said to them, "Do not be amazed! You seek Jesus of Nazareth, the crucified. He has been raised; he is not here. Behold the place where they laid him."

MARK 16:1–6

Standing at the tomb,
I think of you, Lord Jesus.
How many times do we cry
when we stand graveside,
seeking solace in memorials
to those we love.
Transform our grief,
allow us the faith
to see life through death.
Amen.

GRETCHEN L. SCHWENKER

Christ, be with me, Christ before me,
Christ behind me,
Christ in me, Christ beneath me,
Christ above me,
Christ on my right, Christ on my left,
Christ where I lie, Christ where I sit,
Christ where I arise,
Christ in the heart of every one who
thinks of me,
Christ in the mouth of every one who
speaks of me,
Christ in every eye that sees me,
Christ in every ear that hears me.

FROM SAINT PATRICK'S BREASTPLATE

God's Plan

Whatever did not fit in with my plan
did lie within the plan of God.
I have an ever deeper and firmer belief
that nothing is merely an accident
when seen in the light of God,
that my whole life
down to the smallest details
has been marked out for me
in the plan of Divine Providence
and has a completely coherent meaning
in God's all-seeing eyes.
And so I am beginning to rejoice
in the light of glory
wherein this meaning
will be unveiled to me.

SAINT TERESA BENEDICTA OF THE CROSS
(EDITH STEIN)

Are you unaware that we who were baptized into Christ Jesus were baptized into his death? We were indeed buried with him through baptism into death, so that, just as Christ was raised from the dead by the glory of the Father, we too might live in newness of life.

For if we have grown into union with him through a death like his, we shall also be united with him in the resurrection. We know that our old self was crucified with him, so that our sinful body might be done away with, that we might no longer be in slavery to sin. For a dead person has been absolved from sin. If, then, we have died with Christ, we believe that we shall also live with him. We know that Christ, raised from the dead, dies no more; death no longer has power over him.

ROMANS 6:3–9

Let me take solace, God,
knowing that my beloved dead
live in newness of life.
Baptized into your Son's death,
they are united with him
through his sacrifice.
Freed from every sin,
death is no more,
only your glory shines.
For us who remain,
give us abundant faith
that we all find new life in you.

GRETCHEN L. SCHWENKER

The Holy Cross

The Cross is my sure salvation.
The Cross I ever adore.
The Cross of my Lord is with me.
The Cross is my refuge.
Amen.

SAINT THOMAS AQUINAS

Fix thou our steps, O Lord, that we stagger not at the uneven motions of the world, but steadily go on to our glorious home; neither censuring our journey by the weather we meet with, nor turning out of the way for anything that befalls us.

The winds are often rough, and our own weight presses us downwards. Reach forth, O Lord, thy hand, thy saving hand, and speedily deliver us.

Teach us, O Lord, to use this transitory life as pilgrims returning to their beloved home; that we may take what our journey requires, and not think of settling in a foreign country.

AUTHOR UNKNOWN

Remember Jesus Christ, raised from the dead, a descendant of David: such is my gospel, for which I am suffering, even to the point of chains, like a criminal. But the word of God is not chained. Therefore, I bear with everything for the sake of those who are chosen, so that they too may obtain the salvation that is in Christ Jesus, together with eternal glory. This saying is trustworthy: If we have died with him

we shall also live with him;
if we persevere

we shall also reign with him.

2 TIMOTHY 2:8–12A

Dear Lord, whatever chains us,
you make us free in your love.
We are at last free of sin,
leaving suffering and illness
to join you in your reign.
This is my prayer in grief,
that I may live in your promise
of salvation and eternal glory.
That my beloved dead live with you,
that at the end of my life,
I also will live with you
to see again all whom I hold dear.
Amen.

GRETCHEN L. SCHWENKER

See what love the Father has bestowed on us that we may be called the children of God. Yet so we are. The reason the world does not know us is that it did not know him. Beloved, we are God's children now; what we shall be has not yet been revealed. We do know that when it is revealed we shall be like him, for we shall see him as he is.

1 JOHN 3:1–2

You have shown your love,
God, our heavenly Father,
through the gift of your Son.
When he gave his life for us,
we became your children,
who seek to know you.
Help us to always remember,
even in times of sadness,
that we belong to you.
In faith we follow Christ,
so we shall be transformed,
at last becoming like him.
Now and forever.
Amen.

GRETCHEN L. SCHWENKER

Almighty, eternal, just, and merciful God,
grant us in our misery [the grace]
    to do for You alone
        what we know You want us to do,
        and always
    to desire what pleases You.
Thus,
    inwardly cleansed,
    interiorly enlightened,
    and inflamed by the fire of the Holy Spirit,
may we be able to follow
    in the footprints of Your beloved Son,
    our Lord Jesus Christ.
And,
by Your grace alone,
may we make our way to You,
    Most High,
    Who live and rule
      in perfect Trinity and simple Unity,
    and are glorified
      God all-powerful
    forever and ever.
Amen.

SAINT FRANCIS OF ASSISI

⌒ Last Words ⌒

My Lord, it is time to move on.
Well, then, may your will be done.
O my Lord and my Spouse,
The hour that I have longed for has come.
It is time for us to meet one another.
Amen.

SAINT TERESA OF ÁVILA

EPILOGUE

To close this small book of prayers, we visit the stages of loss outlined by Elisabeth Kübler-Ross: denial, anger, bargaining, depression, and acceptance.

Control is a slippery word. We can make career plans and have them derailed by a failing economy. We eat well and exercise and are diagnosed with lung cancer. Carefully constructed equations designed to deliver success and happiness meet the variables of life and we learn that control is an illusion.

As these upheavals interrupt, our brain begins to look for reasons why life is not going as planned. Denial is a hard-wired coping mechanism. If we ignore the loss—what's causing us pain—we think it will disappear. But it does not.

Now that we are waking up in the morning with new loss, we have to make adjustments. No one has prepared us for this loss, and we feel ill-equipped to move forward. Feeling lonely and confused, we do not know how to spend our time or where we might direct our energies. Loneliness is a constant companion, even in the midst of a group who cares for us. With so much disruption, we now find anger. Why did this have to happen to me? It wasn't supposed to work out this way. Anger can invade the smallest parts of our lives, and it surfaces on a daily basis. Patience with the process is needed most at this time.

With the injection of anger in our lives, we begin to bargain. We substitute work for personal reflection; we rationalize routines long after they have served their purpose and avoid exploring new opportunities. We promise to change our behavior so we can return to the way things were. Bargaining is an inward movement of energy and lays the path for the next stage—depression.

Depression has many faces and includes a lack of interest and ability to engage in work and relationships. The smallest decisions seem insurmountable. Depressive behaviors, however, bring us to the point of confronting our loss. The path through depression requires times of isolation and separation, balanced with tears and conversation. The common experience of suffering can help us avoid the inward spiral of anger and direct us outward toward others. In a small way we accept that we do not have ultimate control of our existence, and even our choices, while fully ours, are not protected from clashing with the cycles of life

> *The measurement of when one passes from one stage to the next is made after reflecting candidly on our ability to engage in relationships and on one's emotional, spiritual, and physical condition.*

and death. Little by little life becomes more organized. A silver lining to depression teaches that anyone who has experienced its crippling effects has developed a great capacity to sense the suffering in others.

Acceptance is like stretching muscles that have been underused. We are fragile, yet more resilient than we thought. Yes, it was an ordeal of body and soul. It has brought us closer to our humanity. We now accept limitations and remind ourselves of God's love for us. This acceptance also extends outward, and upon passing through our loss, we are able to envision a new future. We will remember our loved ones with sadness but with less pain. This future includes change—letting go of what was to grasp what may be—and it lets our heart direct our mind to a new place.

Appendix

Praying With the Church

Worshiping together in community is central to our life of faith. Among the many traditional prayers we can recite together are litanies—ancient prayers that go back in time to the earliest days of the Church. We call on God and all holy men and women through these prayers in a communal spirit of gratitude, while also asking for support, comfort, and compassion. The petitions, or invocations, of a litany are recited or sung, and the community repeats a response for each. It is a dialogue between heaven and earth.

Several litanies are provided here to be

prayed as meditation. In the rhythm of their repetitive responses we can find another way to open our hearts to God's presence. Within the richness of every one of these litanies is a connection to the wider Church and most importantly to God the Father, through his Son, Jesus, and in the Holy Spirit.

Litany of the Saints

Lord, have mercy. *Lord, have mercy.*
Christ, have mercy. *Christ, have mercy.*
Lord, have mercy. *Lord, have mercy.*

Holy Mary, Mother of God, *pray for us.*
Saint Michael, *pray for us.*
Holy angels of God, *pray for us.*
Saint John the Baptist, *pray for us.*
Saint Joseph, *pray for us.*
Saints Peter and Paul, *pray for us.*
Saint Andrew, *pray for us.*
Saint John, *pray for us.*
Saint Mary Magdalene, *pray for us.*
Saint Stephen, *pray for us.*
Saint Ignatius of Antioch, *pray for us.*
Saint Lawrence, *pray for us.*
Saints Perpetua and Felicity, *pray for us.*
Saint Agnes, *pray for us.*
Saint Gregory, *pray for us.*
Saint Augustine, *pray for us.*

Saint Athanasius, *pray for us.*
Saint Basil, *pray for us.*
Saint Martin, *pray for us.*
Saint Benedict, *pray for us.*
Saints Francis and Dominic, *pray for us.*
Saint Francis Xavier, *pray for us.*
Saint John Vianney, *pray for us.*
Saint Catherine, *pray for us.*
Saint Teresa of Jesus, *pray for us.*
All holy men and women, *pray for us.*

Lord, be merciful. *Lord, deliver us, we pray.*
From all evil. *Lord, deliver us, we pray.*
From every sin. *Lord, deliver us, we pray.*
From everlasting death. *Lord, deliver us, we pray.*
By your coming as man. *Lord, deliver us, we pray.*
By your death and rising to new life.
   Lord, deliver us, we pray.
By your gift of the Holy Spirit.
   Lord, deliver us, we pray.

Be merciful to us sinners.

Lord, we ask you, hear our prayer.

Guide and protect your holy Church.

Lord, we ask you, hear our prayer.

Keep the pope and all the clergy in faithful
service to your Church.

Lord, we ask you, hear our prayer.

Bring all peoples together in trust and peace.

Lord, we ask you, hear our prayer.

Strengthen us in your service.

Lord, we ask you, hear our prayer.

Jesus, Son of the living God.

Lord, we ask you, hear our prayer.

Christ, hear us. *Christ, hear us.*
Christ, graciously hear us.

Christ, graciously hear us.

Let us pray. God of our ancestors who set their hearts on you, of those who fell asleep in peace, and of those who won the martyrs' violent crown: we are surrounded by these witnesses as by clouds of fragrant incense. In this age we would be counted in this communion of all the saints; keep us always in their good and blessed company. In their midst we make every prayer through Christ who is our Lord forever and ever. *Amen.*

Litany of Saint Joseph

Lord, have mercy on us. *Lord, have mercy on us.*
Lord, have mercy on us. Christ, hear us.
  Christ, graciously hear us.

God, the Father in heaven, *have mercy on us.*
God the Son, Redeemer of the world,
  have mercy on us.
God, the Holy Spirit, *have mercy on us.*
Holy Trinity, one God, *have mercy on us.*

Holy Mary, *pray for us.*
Holy Joseph, *pray for us.*
Noble son of David, *pray for us.*
Light of the patriarchs, *pray for us.*
Spouse of the Mother of God, *pray for us.*
Chaste guardian of the Virgin, *pray for us.*
Foster father of the Son of God, *pray for us.*
Valiant defender of Christ, *pray for us.*
Head of the Holy Family, *pray for us.*
Joseph most just, *pray for us.*
Joseph most chaste, *pray for us.*

Joseph most prudent, *pray for us.*
Joseph most valiant, *pray for us.*
Joseph most obedient, *pray for us.*
Joseph most faithful, *pray for us.*
Mirror of patience, *pray for us.*
Lover of poverty, *pray for us.*
Model of workers, *pray for us.*
Ornament of domestic life, *pray for us.*
Protector of virgins, *pray for us.*
Pillar of families, *pray for us.*
Consolation of the afflicted, *pray for us.*
Hope of the sick, *pray for us.*
Patron of the dying, *pray for us.*
Terror of the demons, *pray for us.*
Protector of the holy Church, *pray for us.*
Lamb of God, who takes away the sins of the world, *spare us, O Lord.*
Lamb of God, who takes away the sins of the world, *graciously hear us, O Lord.*
Lamb of God, who takes away the sins of the world, *have mercy on us, O Lord.*
He gave him charge of his household.
And command over all his goods.

Let us pray. O God, in your providence you chose blessed Joseph to be the spouse of your most holy Mother. Grant, we implore you, that we may have him, whom we venerate on earth, as our protector in heaven. Who lives and reigns world without end. Amen.

Litany of Divine Providence

Lord, have mercy on us. *Christ, have mercy on us.*
Lord, have mercy on us. Christ, hear us.

Christ, graciously hear us.

God the Father of Heaven, *have mercy on us.*

God the Son, Redeemer of the world,

have mercy on us.

God the Holy Spirit, *have mercy on us.*

Holy Trinity, one God, *have mercy on us.*

God, all-knowing and all-wise, *have mercy on us.*

God, all-powerful and all-good, *have mercy on us.*

God, most patient and most merciful,

have mercy on us.

Father of mercy and consolation, *have mercy on us.*

God, wonderful and inscrutable in your plans,

have mercy on us.

God in Whose hands is our life, *have mercy on us.*

God, from whom all good things and every

perfect gift comes, *have mercy on us.*

You who have made all things for the service of

humanity, *have mercy on us.*

You who govern all with wisdom and love,
have mercy on us.

You who fill all living things with blessing,
have mercy on us.

You who clothe the lilies of the field and feed the
birds of the air, *have mercy on us.*

You who number the hairs of our head,
have mercy on us.

You who see in secret, *have mercy on us.*

You who make the sun to shine upon the good
and the bad, *have mercy on us.*

You who call it to rain upon the just and the
unjust, *have mercy on us.*

You who work all things for the benefit of those
who love you, *have mercy on us.*

You who send temporal sufferings for our
correction and good, *have mercy on us.*

You who reward Christian patience with an
eternal reward, *have mercy on us.*

God, our sole refuge and hope, *have mercy on us.*

God, our only consoler and helper,
have mercy on us.

Be merciful, *Spare us, O Lord.*
Be merciful, *Graciously hear us, O Lord.*

From all evil, *deliver us, O Lord.*
From all sin, *deliver us, O Lord.*
From all murmurings and complaints against
    your holy decrees, *deliver us, O Lord.*
From mistrust in your divine Providence,
    deliver us, O Lord.
From too great a trust in riches and the favor of
    people, *deliver us, O Lord.*
From immoderate concern for temporal things,
    deliver us, O Lord.
From misuse or neglect of your gifts and benefits,
    deliver us, O Lord.
From ingratitude toward your loving kindness,
    deliver us, O Lord.
From uncharitableness toward our neighbor,
    deliver us, O Lord.
From stubbornness in sin, *deliver us, O Lord.*
From all dangers of body and soul,
    deliver us, O Lord.

From your well-merited chastisements,
deliver us, O Lord.
From earthquake, pestilence, famine and distress,
deliver us, O Lord.
From disease, hunger and war, *deliver us, O Lord.*
From a wicked and painful death,
deliver us, O Lord.
On the Day of Judgment, *deliver us, O Lord.*

We sinners, *beseech you, hear us.*
That we may always trust in your divine
Providence, *we beseech you, hear us.*
That in good fortune we may not become proud
and godless, *we beseech you, hear us.*
That in misfortune we may not become discour-
aged and impatient, *we beseech you, hear us.*
That we may submit simply to all your decrees,
we beseech you, hear us.
That we may praise your name whether you give
or take away, *we beseech you, hear us.*
That your will may be done on earth as it is in
Heaven, *we beseech you, hear us.*

That we may seek consolation from you in time of trial, *we beseech you, hear us.*

That you may give us what is necessary for the support of our life, *we beseech you, hear us.*

That in all adversities we may grow in patience and humility, *we beseech you, hear us.*

That you may accompany all our labors with your blessing, *we beseech you, hear us.*

That you may reward our temporal sufferings with eternal joys, *we beseech you, hear us.*

That you may fill our spiritual and civil leaders with the spirit of truth and the fear of God, *we beseech you, hear us.*

That you may pity all who suffer want, *we beseech you, hear us.*

That you may console and raise up all the abandoned and oppressed, *we beseech you, hear us.*

That you may reward our benefactors with eternal goods, *we beseech you, hear us.*

That we may praise and glorify your divine Providence now and forever, *we beseech you, hear us.*

Lamb of God, Who takes away the sins of the
world, *spare us, O Lord.*
Lamb of God, Who takes away the sins of the
world, *graciously hear us, O Lord.*
Lamb of God, Who takes away the sins of the
world, *have mercy on us.*

Christ, hear us. *Christ, graciously hear us.*
Lord, have mercy on us. *Christ, have mercy on us.*
Lord, have mercy on us.

Our Father *(silently)*. Hail Mary *(silently)*.

All eyes are turned to you, O Lord,
   and you give them food in season.
You open your gentle hand,
   and fill with blessing all living things.
Lord, show us your mercy,
   and grant us your salvation.

Let us pray. O God, Whose Providence is never
frustrated in its decrees, we beseech you to keep
from us all harm and grant us every blessing,
through Jesus Christ our Lord. *Amen.*

Litany of the Most Holy Trinity

Blessed be the holy Trinity and undivided Unity;
We will give glory to Him, because He has shown His
mercy to us.

O Lord our Lord, how wonderful is your Name
in all the earth!
O the depth of the riches of the wisdom and of the
knowledge of God!

Lord, have mercy. *Lord, have mercy.*
Christ, have mercy. *Christ, have mercy.*
Lord, have mercy. *Lord, have mercy.*
Blessed Trinity, hear us.
Adorable Unity, graciously hear us.

God the Father of Heaven, *have mercy on us.*
God the Son, Redeemer of the world,
have mercy on us.
God the Holy Spirit, *have mercy on us.*

Holy Trinity, One God, *have mercy on us.*

Father from Whom are all things, *have mercy on us.*

Son through Whom are all things,

have mercy on us.

Holy Spirit in Whom are all things,

have mercy on us.

Holy and undivided Trinity, *have mercy on us.*

Father everlasting, *have mercy on us.*

Only-begotten Son of the Father, *have mercy on us.*

Spirit Who proceeds from the Father and the

Son, *have mercy on us.*

Co-eternal Majesty of Three Divine Persons,

have mercy on us.

Father, the Creator, *have mercy on us.*

Son, the Redeemer, *have mercy on us.*

Holy Spirit, the Comforter, *have mercy on us.*

Holy, holy, holy, Lord God of hosts,

have mercy on us.

Who are, Who was, and Who is to come,

have mercy on us.

God Most High, Who inhabits eternity,

have mercy on us.

To Whom alone are due all honor and glory,
have mercy on us.
Who alone does great wonders, *have mercy on us.*
Power infinite, *have mercy on us.*
Wisdom incomprehensible, *have mercy on us.*
Love unspeakable, *have mercy on us.*

Be merciful, *spare us, O Holy Trinity.*
Be merciful, *graciously hear us, O Holy Trinity.*

From all evil, *deliver us, O Holy Trinity.*
From all sin, *deliver us, O Holy Trinity.*
From all pride, *deliver us, O Holy Trinity.*
From all love of riches, *deliver us, O Holy Trinity.*
From all uncleanness, *deliver us, O Holy Trinity.*
From all sloth, *deliver us, O Holy Trinity.*
From all inordinate affection,
deliver us, O Holy Trinity.
From all envy and malice, *deliver us, O Holy Trinity.*
From all anger and impatience,
deliver us, O Holy Trinity.

From every thought, word, and deed contrary to
your holy law, *deliver us, O Holy Trinity.*

Through your almighty power,
deliver us, O Holy Trinity.

Through your plentiful loving kindness,
deliver us, O Holy Trinity.

Through the exceeding treasure of your
goodness and love, *deliver us, O Holy Trinity.*

Through the depths of your wisdom and
knowledge, *deliver us, O Holy Trinity.*

Through all your unspeakable perfections,
deliver us, O Holy Trinity.

We sinners *beseech you, hear us.*

That we may ever serve you alone,
we beseech you, hear us.

That we may worship you in spirit and in truth,
we beseech you, hear us.

That we may love you with all our heart, with all
our soul, and with all our strength,
we beseech you, hear us.

That, for your sake, we may love our neighbor as ourselves, *we beseech you, hear us.*

That we may faithfully keep your holy Commandments, *we beseech you, hear us.*

That we may never defile our bodies and souls with sin, *we beseech you, hear us.*

That we may go from grace to grace, and from virtue to virtue, *we beseech you, hear us.*

That we may finally enjoy the sight of you in glory, *we beseech you, hear us.*

That you would hear us, *we beseech you, hear us.*

O Blessed Trinity, *we beseech you, deliver us.*
O Blessed Trinity, *we beseech you, save us.*
O Blessed Trinity, *have mercy on us.*
Lord, have mercy, *Christ, have mercy.*
Lord, have mercy, *Christ, have mercy.*

Our Father *(silently)*. Hail Mary *(silently)*.

Blessed are You, O Lord, in the firmament of
Heaven
*and worthy to be praised, and glorious, and
highly exalted forever.*

Let us pray. Almighty and everlasting God, Who
has granted your servants in the confession of
the True Faith, to acknowledge the glory of and
Eternal Trinity, and in the power of your majesty
to adore a Unity: we beseech you that by the
strength of this faith we may be defended from
all adversity. Through Jesus Christ our Lord.
Amen.

Litany of
Saint Martin de Porres

Lord, have mercy on us. *Christ, have mercy on us.*

Lord, have mercy on us. Christ, hear us.

> *Christ, graciously hear us.*

God the Father of Heaven, *have mercy on us.*

God the Son, Redeemer of the world,

> *have mercy on us.*

God the Holy Spirit, *have mercy on us.*

Holy Trinity, One God, *have mercy on us.*

Holy Mary, Queen of the Most Holy Rosary,

> *pray for us.*

Saint Martin, ever in the presence of God,

> *pray for us.*

Saint Martin, faithful servant of Christ,

> *pray for us.*

Saint Martin, lover of the Holy Eucharist,

> *pray for us.*

Saint Martin, devoted to our Blessed Mother,

> *pray for us.*

Saint Martin, spiritual patron of Americans, *pray for us.*

Saint Martin, raised from the depths to a heavenly mansion, *pray for us.*

Saint Martin, honored son of Saint Dominic, *pray for us.*

Saint Martin, lover of the Most Holy Rosary, *pray for us.*

Saint Martin, apostle of mercy, *pray for us.*

Saint Martin, winged minister of charity, *pray for us.*

Saint Martin, miraculously conveyed to far-distant lands, *pray for us.*

Saint Martin, freed from the barriers of time and space, *pray for us.*

Saint Martin, seeking the conversion of sinners, *pray for us.*

Saint Martin, protector of the tempted and repentant, *pray for us.*

Saint Martin, helper of souls in doubt and darkness, *pray for us.*

Saint Martin, compassionate to the sorrowful
and afflicted, *pray for us.*

Saint Martin, consoler of the discouraged and
unfortunate, *pray for us.*

Saint Martin, peacemaker in all discords,
pray for us.

Saint Martin, touched by all suffering, *pray for us.*

Saint Martin, comforter of the sick and dying,
pray for us.

Saint Martin, angel to hospitals and prisons,
pray for us.

Saint Martin, worker of miraculous cures,
pray for us.

Saint Martin, guardian of the homeless child,
pray for us.

Saint Martin, humbly hiding God-given powers,
pray for us.

Saint Martin, devoted to holy poverty, *pray for us.*

Saint Martin, model of obedience, *pray for us.*

Saint Martin, lover of heroic penance, *pray for us.*

Saint Martin, strong in self-denial, *pray for us.*

Saint Martin, performing menial tasks with holy ardor, *pray for us.*

Saint Martin, gifted with prophecy, *pray for us.*

Saint Martin, symbol of interracial brotherhood, *pray for us.*

Lamb of God, Who takes away the sins of the world, *spare us, O Lord.*

Lamb of God, Who takes away the sins of the world, *graciously hear us, O Lord.*

Lamb of God, Who takes away the sins of the world, *have mercy on us.*

Pray for us, Saint Martin,
that we may be made worthy of the promises of Christ.

Let us pray. O God, the exalter of the humble, who made Saint Martin, your confessor, to enter the heavenly kingdom, grant through his merits and intercession that we may so follow the example of his humility on earth as to deserve to be exalted with him in Heaven, through Christ our Lord. *Amen.*

CREDITS

HEAR OUR PRAYER

"To choose life..." from *Theology for Skeptics* by Dorothee Soelle. Copyright © 1995 by Augsburg Fortress Publishers, Minneapolis, Minnesota.

"O merciful God, who answerest the poor..." Day of Atonement (Yom Kippur). The *Oxford Book of Prayer*, edited by George Appleton. New York: Oxford University Press, Inc., 1985.

"Memorare." *The Essential Catholic Prayer Book: A Collection of Private and Community Prayers.* Liguori, MO: Liguori Publications, 1999.

"Our Father, You would not willingly call on us to suffer..." by Saint Elizabeth Ann Seton (1774–1821). Courtesy, Daughters of Charity Archives, Emmitsburg, Maryland. Originally from 8.7 "O tarry thou thy Lord's leisure..." 26 July 1801, Regina Bechtle, S.C., and Judith Metz, S.C., eds., Ellin M. Kelly, mss. ed., *Elizabeth Bayley Seton Collected Writings*, 3 vols. (2000–2006), 3a:.20. Used with permission.

"Oh Lord, you have made us very small..." from *Justice and Mercy* (rev.) by Reinhold Niebuhr (Harper & Row, 1974, ed. Ursula Niebuhr).

"O my God! I ask of you for myself..." by Saint Thérèse of Lisieux (1873–1897) and "Govern all by your wisdom..." by Saint Teresa of Ávila (1515–1582). *Praying with the Saints: Making Their Prayers Your Own.* Edited by Woodeene Koenig-Bricker. Chicago: Loyola Press, 2001.

"Christ our eternal King and God..." *The Divine Liturgy of St. John Chrysostom.* From N. M. Vaporis, ed. *An Orthodox Prayer Book/Mikron Euchologion* (Brookline, MA: Holy Cross Orthodox Press, 1977). Used with permission.

"Oh Holy Spirit, come into my heart..." by Saint Catherine of Siena (1347–1380). Prayer 6, *The Prayers of Catherine of Siena,* translated and edited by Suzanne Noffke, OP. San Jose: Authors Choice Press, 2001. Used with permission.

EVERY TEAR WILL BE WIPED AWAY

"The real lesson of resurrection..." from *In Search of Belief,* rev. ed. by Joan Chittister. Copyright © 2006 Liguori Publications.

"Morning Prayers" reprinted with the permission of Scribner, a Division of Simon & Schuster, Inc., from LETTERS AND PAPERS FROM PRISON, REVISED, ENLARGED ED. by Dietrich Bonhoeffer, translated from the German by R.H. Fuller, Frank Clark, et al.

Copyright © 1953, 1967, 1971 by SCM Press Ltd. All rights reserved.

"Watch, dear Lord..." by Saint Augustine (354–450) and "O God, you care for your creation..." by Dimma, seventh-century Irish monk. *The Essential Catholic Prayer Book: A Collection of Private and Community Prayers.* Liguori, MO: Liguori Publications, 1999.

"For Healing," www.ourcatholicfaith.org. "A Prayer for Healing," Priests and Brothers of the Sacred Heart, Sacred Heart Monastery, Hales Corners, WI, USA.

"O Lord Jesus Christ..." from *Annus Domini: A Prayer for Each Day of the Year, Founded on a Text of Holy Scripture* (1874) by Christina Rossetti.

"Lord, Jesus Christ" from *Listening to Your Life: Daily Meditations with Frederick Buechner.* HarperSanFrancisco, 1992. Copyright © 1992 by Frederick Buechner. Reprinted with permission by Frederick Buechner Literary Assets, LLC.

MAY ANGELS LEAD YOU INTO PARADISE

"Heaven knows terrible things happen..." from *The Magnificent Defeat* by Frederick Buechner. Copyright © 1966 by Frederick Buechner. Copyright renewed 1994 by Frederick Buechner. Reprinted by permission of HarperCollins Publishers.

"Kontakion 9" and "Ikos 9," from *Book of Akathists: To Our Saviour the Mother of God and Various Saints,* Vol. 1 (Jordanville, New York: Holy Trinity Monastery, 1994). Used with permission.

"I am going now into the sleep," *The Oxford Book of Prayer,* edited by George Appleton. New York: Oxford University Press, Inc., 1985.

"O bodiless Angels..." from *Lord, I Call.* Reprinted with permission from Orthodox Church in America, www.oca.org.

"In paradisum" ("Into Paradise"). Antiphon, Latin Liturgy, Requiem Mass. Rite of Gathering in the Presence of the Body, *Order of Christian Funerals.* English translation, *The Essential Catholic Prayer Book: A Collection of Private and Community Prayers.* Liguori, MO: Liguori Publications, 1999.

"Are they not all Ministering Spirits?" from *The Complete Poems of Christina Rossetti* (London: 1888, 1890) by Christina Rossetti.

"Welcome into Heaven" and "Anima Christi" (fourteenth century). *The Essential Catholic Prayer Book: A Collection of Private and Community Prayers.* Liguori, MO: Liguori Publications, 1999.

"As the rain hides the stars..." Gaelic prayer, Alistair MacLean, trans. *The Oxford Book of Prayer,* edited by George Appleton. New York: Oxford University Press, Inc., 1985.

GLORY OF ALL BELIEVERS

"The Freedom of Christians" from *Foundations of Christian Faith: An Introduction to the Idea of Christianity* by Karl Rahner. Copyright © 1982 by Crossroad Publishing Company. Reproduced with permission of Crossroad Publishing Company in the format Tradebook via Copyright Clearance Center.

"Prayer of Solace." *The Armed Forces Prayer Book.* New York; Protestant Episcopal Church, 1951. Used with permission.

"Kontakion 12" and "Ikos 12," from *Book of Akathists: To Our Saviour the Mother of God and Various Saints,* Vol. 1 (Jordanville, New York: Holy Trinity Monastery, 1994). Used with permission.

"Saint Patrick's Breastplate" (Saint Patrick, 390–461; inscribed in the Book of Armagh, early ninth century). *The Oxford Book of Prayer,* edited by George Appleton. New York: Oxford University Press, Inc., 1985.

"God's Plan" by Saint Teresa Benedicta of the Cross (Edith Stein, 1891–1942). *Praying with the Saints: Making Their Prayers Your Own.* Edited by Woodeene Koenig-Bricker. Chicago: Loyola Press, 2001.

"Good Lord, give me the grace..." by Saint Thomas More (1478–1535) and "The Holy Cross" by Saint Thomas Aquinas (ca. 1225–1274). *The Essential Catholic Prayer*

Book: A Collection of Private and Community Prayers. Liguori, MO: Liguori Publications, 1999.

"Fix thou our steps, O Lord..." Author unknown. *The Book of Jesus.* Edited by Calvin Miller. New York: Simon & Schuster, 1996.

"Almighty, eternal, just, and merciful God..." Excerpts from *Francis and Clare: The Complete Works,* translated and introduced by Regis J. Armstrong, OFM, CAP, and Ignatius C. Brady, OFM, Copyright © 1982 by Paulist Press, Inc. New York/Mahwah, NJ. Reprinted by permission of Paulist Press, Inc. www.paulistpress.com.

"Last Words" by Saint Teresa of Ávila (1515–1582). *The Essential Catholic Prayer Book: A Collection of Private and Community Prayers.* Liguori, MO: Liguori Publications, 1999.

APPENDIX

"Litany of the Saints" from *Catholic Household Blessings & Prayers,* rev. ed. Washington, DC: Bishop's Committee on the Liturgy, United States Conference of Catholic Bishops, 2007.

"Litany of Saint Joseph" from *The Essential Catholic Prayer Book: A Collection of Private and Community Prayers.* Liguori, MO: Liguori Publications, 1999.

"Litany of Divine Providence," "Litany of the Most Holy Trinity," and "Litany of Saint Martin de Porres," from *A Prayerbook of Favorite Litanies: 116 Catholic Litanies and Responsory Prayers.* Compiled by Fr. Albert J. Hebert, S.M. Tan Books and Publishers, 1985.